D0230950

Ways into Science

Seasons

Written by Peter Riley

W
FRANKLIN WATTS
LONDON • SYDNEY

This edition 2008

Franklin Watts
338 Euston Road, London NW1 3BH

Franklin Watts Australia
Level 17/207 Kent Street
Sydney, NSW 2000

Copyright text © Peter Riley 2003
Copyright images © Franklin Watts 2003

Series editor: Sarah Peutrill
Art director: Jonathan Hair
Design: Ian Thompson
Photography: Ray Moller (unless otherwise credited)
Photo researcher: Diana Morris

A CIP catalogue record for this book is
available from the British Library

ISBN 978 0 7496 8335 1

Printed in Malaysia

Picture Credits:
J & M Bain/NHPA front cover cl & p.17; Ian Beames/Ecoscene/Papilio p.
15; Ray Bird/FLPA p. 14; Frank Blackburn/Ecoscene/Papilio p. 20b;
H.D.Brand/FLPA p. 12tr; Michael Callan/FLPA: front cover bl & p. 23t;
G.J.Cambridge/NHPA p. 18t; Laurie Campbell/NHPA: front cover br &
p.18cl; Hugh Clark/FLPA p. 25; Anthony Cooper/Ecoscene/Papilio p. 10;
Peter Currell/Ecoscene/Papilio p. 24; Geoff du Feu/Bubbles P.L p. 9t; Don
Gray/Photofusion p. 8b; David Hosking/FLPA p. 13b; S & D & K
Maslowski/FLPA pp. 6, 7; Sally Morgan/Ecoscene/Papilio p. 20t;
J.Watkins/FLPA p. 12c; Ian West/Bubbles P.L p. 16; L.West/FLPA pp.
18cr, 23b; Terry Whittaker/FLPA p. 12b; R. Wilmshurst/FLPA p. 11; Ken
Wilson/Ecoscene/Papilio front cover cr & pp.13t, 21t, 21c,22t;
M.B.Withers/FLPA p.12tl

Whilst every attempt has been made to clear copyright should there be
an inadvertent omission please apply in the first instance to the publisher
regarding rectification.

To my granddaughter Megan Kate

Franklin Watts is a division of Hachette Children's Books,
an Hachette Livre UK company.

Contents

Four  seasons

In many parts of the world there are four seasons.

Spring

Summer

Autumn

Winter

Which season is it now?

Weather

In every season the weather can change from day to day.

There are cloudy and wet days all year round, but usually fewer of them in summer.

There are sunny days any time of year. A sunny day in winter is cold, but in summer it is hot.

8

It can be windy any time but the wind blows stronger in autumn or spring.

We only get snow in winter or early spring.

What is the weather like today?

Spring

As winter changes to spring, the days get longer and the weather is warmer. It rains a lot.

New plants start to grow.

Some new animal life also begins in spring.

Birds make nests and lay eggs.

What do you think happens to the eggs? Turn the page to find out.

Summer

In summer the eggs hatch.

The chicks are taught to find food. They grow and leave the nest.

Other young animals, such as otters, are also taught to find food.

Many plants have flowers in summer. Insects carry pollen between the flowers, so the flowers make fruits and seeds.

What do you think these flowers will change into when the petals drop off? Turn the page to find out.

Autumn

In autumn the flowers grow into fruits called berries.

The fruits contain seeds, which will make new plants in the spring.

In autumn some animals prepare for winter.
Squirrels gather food to eat in the winter.

Winter

In the winter birds sometimes cannot find enough food to eat.

Sophie is putting out food for them.

Can you find a place to feed the birds in winter?

Many plants need lots of warmth and light to grow properly. In the cold, dark winter they stop growing.

Seeds, bulbs and roots lie in the soil protected from cold weather. They begin to shoot again as the winter ends.

Turn the page to find out what happens to this plant next.

In spring and summer the extra heat and light make plants grow.

In autumn berries grow. The leaves die back.

In winter the roots stay alive in the cold, dark soil.

18

Tom is trying a test to see why bulbs grow shoots in the spring.

He puts an onion bulb in a warm place.

After a few days roots appear.

What do you think happens when he puts an onion bulb in a cold place?

Some trees, like the holly and pine, keep their leaves all year round.

The holly has spiky leaves. It has red berries in the autumn and winter.

The pine has long thin leaves like needles. It has cones which hold its seeds.

20

Some trees lose their leaves each year.

In autumn, this tree's leaves turn brown and start to fall off.

By the winter, all the leaves have fallen off.

What do you think happens to this tree in the spring? Turn the page to find out.

The tree makes new leaves in the spring. The mild weather and spring rain help leaves to grow.

Emily puts a twig with some buds on in a jar of water. She marks the water level.

What do you think happens? Try Emily's test and look at the water level every day.

Some animals change through the year as well.

Deer grow thick fur in the winter to keep them warm. It thins out again in late spring.

In summer, some birds lose their worn-out feathers. This is called moulting. They soon grow new ones.

Some birds join up in flocks in autumn.
They fly away to a warmer place for the winter.

In spring they return again.

This is called migration.

Have you seen any flocks of birds in autumn?

Some animals sleep through the winter. We say they hibernate.

This bat has found a safe place to hibernate through the winter.

The bat will wake up in the spring when there are more insects flying around and food is easier to find.

Harry records the weather in each season. For five days in January, April, July and October he does three things:

1. Checks if sky is clear or cloudy. (You must never look at the Sun.)

2. Finds out how warm or cold it is.

26

3. Measures the rain.

He writes the results in a table.

Month: July			Season: summer
day	sky	temperature (°C)	rain (mm)
1	clear	20	0
2	cloudy	15	2
3			
4			
5			

Record the weather in different seasons like Harry.

Useful Words

bulbs: balls made by the stem and leaves of some plants. Bulbs grow into new plants.

chicks: newly hatched birds.

eggs: the early forms of animals such as birds and frogs.

fruits: the parts of plants that hold the seeds.

fur: a thick coat of hair.

hibernate: to sleep through the winter.

migrate: to move to a different place when the weather changes with the seasons.

nests: animal homes made from grass, twigs, or mud.

petals: the parts of a flower that are usually colored.

pollen: a yellow powder that helps flowers make seeds.

roots: the parts of plants that grow into the soil to soak up water. Roots help hold plants in place.

seasons: time periods through the year with weather patterns that change with the temperatures.

seeds: the usually tiny parts made by plants that can grow into new plants.

twigs: small, woody stalks at the ends of branches.

shoots: young plants that have just started to grow from seeds.

Some answers

Here are some answers to the questions we have asked in this book. Don't worry if you had some different answers to ours; you may be right, too. Talk through your answers with other people and see if you can explain why they are right.

Page 9   Your answer may depend on the time of day. You could look at the weather in the morning and afternoon and compare them.

Page 16   If a bird table is set up it must be away from bushes in which cats can hide.

Page 19   Plants need warmth to grow so in a cold place the growth will be much less than in a warm place. The onion bulb will produce shorter roots or may not even produce any roots.

Page 22   The level of water in the jar goes down. The twig bursts into leaf. This is because the twig is taking up water and using it to make new leaf material and to push out the parts already made and stored in the buds.

Page 24   Swallows form flocks in early autumn and migrate. In late autumn flocks of geese may be seen at night moving to winter feeding grounds from their summer breeding grounds. Starlings flock to towns and cities in winter for warmth and a regular supply of food.

Index

About this book

Ways into Science is designed to encourage children to begin to think about their everyday world in a scientific way, examining cause and effect through close observation, recording their results and discussing what they have seen. Here are some pointers to gain the maximum use from **Seasons.**

• Working through this book will introduce the basic concepts about how living things are adapted to survive the different seasons of the year and also some of the language structures and vocabulary associated with them. This will prepare the child for more formal work later in the school curriculum.

• Safety: ensure children do not pick or touch berries as many are poisonous; on page 8 you may wish to discuss the use of sun block and skin care in sunny weather.

• On pages 11, 13 and 21 the children are invited to predict how a living thing changes using their general knowledge. Discuss the reason for any answer they give in some depth. On page 11 look for an answer about the eggs hatching but the children may also mention the parent sitting on them to incubate them. The bird featured has a long incubation period and late nesting season starting in May which takes it into the summer season featured on page 12. Many other birds start nesting earlier and have shorter incubation periods so the eggs may hatch in the spring and the chicks leave the nest before summer. These birds often have two or even three broods of chicks so eggs will be laid and chicks reared throughout spring and summer. On page 13 look for an answer about fruit or berries. On page 21 look for an answer about buds bursting open and new leaves growing out. At the beginning of the activity on pages 26 and 27 you may like the children to make the four tables at once so they realise it will be a long investigation.